DANCING AT LUGHNASA

Brian Friel's
DANCING AT LUGHNASA
Screenplay by
Frank McGuinness

faber and faber

First published in 1998
by Faber and Faber Limited
3 Queen Square London WC1N 3AU

Photoset by Parker Typesetting Service, Leicester
Printed in England by Clays Ltd, St Ives plc

2 4 6 8 10 9 7 5 3 1

For Cissie O Haire

Dancing at Lughnasa

CAST AND CREW

KATE MUNDY	Meryl Streep
FATHER JACK MUNDY	Michael Gambon
CHRISTINA MUNDY	Catherine McCormack
MAGGIE MUNDY	Kathy Burke
ROSE MUNDY	Sophie Thompson
AGNES MUNDY	Brid Brennan
GERRY EVANS	Rhys Ifans
MICHAEL MUNDY	Darrel Johnston
DANNY BRADLEY	Lorcan Cranitch
AUSTIN MORGAN	Peter Gowen
SOPHIA MCLOUGHLIN	Dawn Bradfield
VERA MCLOUGHLIN	Marie Mullen
FATHER CARLIN	John Kavanagh
CHEMIST	Kate O'Toole
NARRATION BY	Gerard McSorley

Choreographer	David Bolger
Financial Controller	Donal Geraghty
Production Manager	Des Martin
First Assistant Director	Robert Quinn
Camera Operator	Des Whelan
Script Supervisor	Libbie Barr
Script Consultant	Judy Friel
Production Co-ordinator	Anneliese O'Callaghan
Casting Director	Mary Selway
Costume Designer	Joan Bergin
Production Designer	Mark Geraghty
Line Producer	Gerrit Folsom
Editor	Humphrey Dixon
Director of Photography	Kenneth MacMillan, B.S.C.
Music by	Bill Whelan
Screenplay by	Frank McGuinness
Based on the original stage play by	Brian Friel
Producer	Noel Pearson
Director	Pat O'Connor

3

EXT. SKY – DAY

A kite, grotesquely decorated by a child's hand, flies in the sky.

EXT. FIELDS – DAY

A boy, Michael, flies the kite skilfully. He looks into the blue sky and the sun.

The sun blinds him.

He lets go of the kite and it flies away.

EXT. SKY – DAY

The kite flies over the landscape of Ulster with people harvesting, leaving behind the boy, the field he stands in and the cottage where the Mundy family live.

Music.

INT. COTTAGE – DAY

The cottage is plainly furnished.

The adult Michael's voice sounds.

> MICHAEL
> (*voice-over*)
> When I cast my mind back to that summer of 1936, different kinds of memories offer themselves to me.

INT. COTTAGE – DAY

A close-up of a wireless, the name Marconi printed clearly on it.

MICHAEL
(*voice-over*)

We got our first wireless set that summer – well, a sort of a set, and it obsessed us. We called him Lugh, after the old pagan god of the harvest, and his festival was Lughnasa, a time of music and dance.

INT. COTTAGE – DAY

A photograph of Father Jack in his prime, as a strong young man, radiant and splendid in his army chaplain's uniform.

MICHAEL
(*voice-over*)

Then my mother's brother, my Uncle Jack, came home from Africa for the first time in twenty-five years. He was the oldest of the family. And the only boy.

INT. KITCHEN – DAY

A cracked mirror, distorting the kitchen. Christina combs her hair, making faces at her reflection.

MICHAEL
(*voice-over*)

That was my mother. How beautiful she was.

CHRISTINA

I'm going to throw this old cracked thing out.

Maggie's face joins Christina in the mirror's reflection.

MAGGIE

You are not.

The camera shows the two women face to face.

The mirror goes.

I broke it. The only way to avoid seven years' bad luck is to keep on using it.

CHRISTINA

Do you know, I think I might just start wearing lipstick.

6

MAGGIE

Steady on, girl. Today it's lipstick. Tomorrow it's the gin bottle.

(*she draws on a cigarette*)

Dear wild Woodbine, better than any man. Not that I'd know. Better not let Kate hear that kind of chat.

EXT. COTTAGE GARDEN – DAY

Kate's face in close-up, firm, determined.

MICHAEL

(*voice-over*)

If Aunt Maggie smoked and took life lightly, Aunt Kate did not. She was a schoolteacher. And a strict one.

EXT. COTTAGE GARDEN – DAY

Agnes is up a ladder, whitewashing a wall.

Kate calls up to her.

KATE

Agnes, what are you doing up there?

7

AGNES

I'm putting the finishing touches to this wall.

KATE

You should have done that yesterday.

AGNES

I want it to look nice for Jack.

KATE

Get yourself ready. Do you want the whole town laughing at us?

AGNES

I've only to pull on a skirt.

KATE

Well, please do so, and do something with your hair as well. Where's Rose?

AGNES

She's feeding the chickens.

KATE

I suppose she looks like a mad woman as well.

Kate storms off.

Agnes glares after her, coming down the ladder.

EXT. COTTAGE GARDEN – DAY

Close-up of Agnes's face.

MICHAEL
(voice-over)

My mother used to whisper, 'Agnes is deep – she says little.'

EXT. COTTAGE GARDEN

Rose is throwing food to chickens.

A white rooster follows her.

EXT. COTTAGE GARDEN – DAY

Close-up of Rose's face.

> MICHAEL
> (*voice-over*)
>
> And that's Aunt Rose. Rose was a bit slow. Simple, that's the
> word we used.

EXT. COTTAGE GARDEN – DAY

Rose lifts her skirt and dances before the rooster.

She sings.

> ROSE
>
> Will you come to Abyssinia, will you come?
> Bring your own cup and saucer and a bun,
> Mussolini will be there –

Kate appears before her.

The rooster runs away in terror.

> KATE
>
> Mussolini is many miles away. Father Jack, your only brother,
> will be in Ballybeg in one hour. Would you please make
> yourself presentable, Rose.

She walks away.

Rose charms the rooster back to her.

She lifts it into her arms.

> ROSE
>
> Don't mind her. She's only an old gander. Gander.

EXT. THE MUNDY FAMILY WALK DOWN A COUNTRY LANE – DAY

> MICHAEL
> (*voice-over*)
>
> And so we set out to meet my Uncle Jack. Little did I know it,
> child as I was, that this was the beginning of things changing,
> changing so quickly, too quickly.

9

EXT. THE VILLAGE OF BALLYBEG – DAY

The Mundy women move through the main street. The eldest, Kate, is at their head. Maggie walks beside her. Agnes and Rose walk behind them, arms linked. Behind them come Christina with her son, the boy Michael. They are wearing their best Sunday clothes, although, from the working people of the village, it is obviously not Sunday. Michael's black boots, although worn, are immaculately polished.

EXT. VILLAGE STREET – DAY

A chemist walks from her store. She speaks to Kate.

> CHEMIST
> Well, Miss Mundy, a big day for yous all. Father Jack, back at long last amongst you.

> KATE
> It is indeed, thank you.

> CHEMIST
> Something for yous all to be proud of.
> *(looking at Michael)*

All that time among the lepers. The man's a saint. Father
Jack's a saint.

                    KATE
Thank you. The bus will be in soon, if you'll excuse us.

                    CHEMIST
Give him our best wishes.

She leaves them.

                    MAGGIE
Give him your arse and say it's parsley.

                    KATE
That's enough, thank you, Margaret.

EXT. ROAD – DAY

A country road.

Shot of bus travelling.

EXT. VILLAGE STREET – DAY

Danny Bradley walks down the other side of the street.

Rose grows excited and whispers to Agnes.

                    ROSE
Look, Agnes. It's Danny Bradley.

                    AGNES
Hold your tongue, Rose.

                    ROSE
Will I run over to say hello?

                    AGNES
You'll stay right here beside me.

Danny Bradley takes off his cap and bows to the sisters.

                    CHRISTINA
Danny Bradley's a scut, Rose.

MAGGIE
With three young children. Everybody in the town knows.

ROSE
And who are you to talk, Christina Mundy! You're jealous,
that's what's wrong with the whole lot of you – you're jealous
of me.

KATE
(*gently*)
Rose, would you please control yourself.

MAGGIE
His wife left him. She did the runner.

KATE
She might have had her reasons.

Rose sees the bus.

ROSE
It's coming. The bus, it's coming.

*Rose grows very excited, shouting and pointing. Kate holds her hand
tightly.*

But the women's excitement is obvious, Kate's as much as the others'.

> KATE
> (*whispers to herself*)
>
> Jack. Thank God, Jack.

EXT. VILLAGE STREET – DAY

The bus arrives. Father Carlin is standing with a group of men.

EXT. VILLAGE STREET – DAY

Father Jack exits from the bus. He is tanned, grey-haired, tired and dazed.

He looks at the women and child waiting to meet him.

Father Carlin watches closely, registers displeasure.

> JACK
>
> Is this – is this –

> KATE
>
> Ballybeg, Jack. Ballybeg.

> JACK
>
> This is the name of where – where –

> KATE
>
> Where you came from, Jack. Your home. In Ireland.

> JACK
>
> Am I home?

> KATE
>
> You are, Jack. You're home. This is Ireland.

He holds out his hand.

> JACK
>
> Mother is dead. She's not here. She's dead.

He starts to cry.

Kate squeezes his hand with one of her hands. She places the other over his mouth.

MICHAEL

He's an old man, Mammy.

Christina repeats Kate's gestures with Michael, squeezing one hand, placing another over his mouth.

The driver carries Jack's luggage off the bus.

A trunk breaks open. It contains a white uniform, a battered hat and a mask whose face resembles the grotesque face on Michael's kite. It falls at Father Carlin's feet as he passes.

EXT. CLOSE-UP OF JACK'S WORN FACE – DAY

EXT. CLOSE-UP OF MICHAEL'S DISAPPOINTED FACE – DAY

INT. COTTAGE – DAY

A photograph of Jack as a young man.

Michael looks at it, puzzled.

INT. COTTAGE – DAY

Maggie's hand switches on the wireless. 'The Homes of Donegal' starts to play. Maggie claps her hands in delight.

INT. COTTAGE – DAY

Jack sits on the bed and listens, enraptured by the music. He rises and goes to the bedroom door. They see him. As the song continues, the women's faces reflect their adoration of Jack.

INT. COTTAGE – DAY

Kate's features are animated, excited.

INT. COTTAGE – DAY

Agnes looks happily from Jack's face to Rose.

INT. COTTAGE – DAY

Rose's face is serious and still.

INT. COTTAGE – DAY

Michael and Christina both sit on Maggie's knees, one on each. She has an arm around both.

INT. COTTAGE – DAY

The music continues and the whole kitchen is seen, its neat and spare furniture. A crucifix hangs on the wall opposite the mirror.

INT. COTTAGE – DAY

The music continues.

The mirror reflects the cracked image of the crucifix.

INT. BEDROOM – DAY

On a window-ledge there is a statue of the Virgin Mary. Beneath it is a vase of red poppies.

17

The bedspread is red. The sheets are immaculately white.

EXT. GARDEN – DAY

The music continues.

A white sheet is being scrubbed ferociously against a washboard in a zinc bath.

EXT. GARDEN – DAY

A spade goes through clay, digging up potatoes.

EXT. GARDEN – DAY

An axe strikes and breaks a block of wood. At the blow of the axe the music stops.

EXT. GARDEN – DAY

Christina wrings the sheet through a mangle.

INT. JACK'S BEDROOM – DAY

Jack is asleep in bed.

EXT. GARDEN – DAY

Agnes is digging the potatoes. Rose following her, puts them into a bucket.

EXT. GARDEN – DAY

Maggie is chopping the wood. Michael piles it into a large basket.

EXT. COTTAGE – EVENING

Light shines from the cottage's windows.

INT. KITCHEN – DAY

Agnes and Rose are knitting gloves, a large batch of them neatly piled on the table.

Kate is reading.

Jack and Michael are fiddling with the radio.

We hear through the radio's cackles the end of a piece of music. A voice sounds from the radio.

VOICE

This is Radio Eireann, broadcasting from Athlone, and remember, if you feel like singing, do sing an Irish song.

Interference sounds deafeningly from the radio. The radio goes dead.

JACK

It's a miracle.

KATE

It's no miracle, Jack. It's science.

ROSE

It's not science, Kate. It's the god of Lughnasa.

MAGGIE

We call this boy Lugh, Jack –

MICHAEL

Because he's the god of music, Uncle Jack, and dancing, and this is his festival.

KATE

Pagan nonsense, celebrating the feast of Lughnasa. This is the month of August, the feast of Our Lady's Assumption into heaven.

JACK

A goddess, rising through the sky and the stars to greet her dear son. Where is Michael's father, Christina?

The women greet the question with silence. Christina breaks it.

CHRISTINA

He's not here.

KATE

They're not married.

JACK

So Michael is a child of love. A son conceived in love. I'm
glad you've had a child conceived in love, Agnes.

AGNES

He's not mine. He's Christina's.

Jack searches among the faces of his sisters.

CHRISTINA

Mine, Jack. He's mine.

JACK

All of you, he belongs to all of you. You all love him.

ROSE

Danny Bradley wants to marry me. He wants to take me up to
the back hills one day, to Lough Anna –

KATE

I will not tell you again, Rose –

ROSE

Will you marry us, Jack?

AGNES

Danny can't marry you, Rose. He's married already. You
know that.

ROSE

But he loves me, Agnes. And I love him. And his wife's left
him.

KATE

That's not our business. It's not our business. Jack, you must
be tired. Have a wee sleep before you eat. It will build up an
appetite, a good sleep.

JACK

In Africa we sleep and dream and the dream we sacrifice to
the gods –

KATE

This is not Africa. This is Ballybeg, Jack. Your home. This is
Donegal. This is Ireland.

The radio blasts music again. It is an orchestra playing 'Anything Goes'.

JACK

Another miracle.

KATE

It's not a miracle. It is science, Jack.

JACK

It's music. Dance with me, mother.

KATE

Turn that off. Turn it off. I'll do it myself.
                    (she turns off the radio)
Jack, I am not mother. I am Kate, your eldest sister. You're going to bed for a short while. The only miracles are those God ordains. And you are an ordained priest. You do not dance. Maggie, see Jack to his rest, if you please.

JACK

Yes, my rest. So many women in Africa had love children and they were loved –

CHRISTINA
(firmly)

As they are here.

JACK

Of course, yes they are. I'm sorry. I upset you. But I would like you all to have a love child –

KATE

His Holiness the Pope would have something to say against that.

JACK

Yes, he would, but he's never lived in Africa.

Maggie is drawing on a Woodbine.

MAGGIE

I'll put you to your bed, Jack. You need a rest. And if His Holiness the Pope doesn't fancy a stay in Africa, I might take

his place. The sisters here can tell you I've been looking for a
beautiful, black man –

                              KATE

Maggie –

                                        MAGGIE

   Come on, Jack, bed. A wee rest.

INT. A BEDROOM – DAY

Two single beds.

Maggie is undressing Jack.

                              JACK

   Thank you, Okawa.

                              MAGGIE

Who's Okawa?

                              JACK

You are.

INT. KITCHEN – DAY

> **KATE**
> I have to laugh at you, Christina Mundy.

> **CHRISTINA**
> Whenever you say you have to laugh at me, Kate, I know you're not laughing.

> **KATE**
> And I have to say that I've to laugh at you, Rose Mundy. A brother home from the foreign missions, a priest, confronted by one sister who's given birth to an illegitimate child –

> **CHRISTINA**
> Michael, go outside and play. Go outside and play.

Michael, puzzled, leaves the kitchen.

Christina takes the boiling kettle from the hob. The steam stings her eyes.

> **KATE**
> And Rose talking about men separated from their wives.

> **ROSE**
> I was talking about Danny Bradley. He loves me. He loves me, Kate.

> **KATE**
> (*roars*)
> Love?

> **ROSE**
> (*roars back*)
> Gander. Gander.

Kate glares at her.

> That's what you're called in your classroom. Gander. You're not even a woman. You're called the gander.

> **KATE**
> I am woman enough to know what modesty is. A woman's modesty is everything.

24

Kate leaves the kitchen.

INT. A BEDROOM – DAY

Now in his pyjamas, Jack lies in the bed, waiting for the sheet to cover him.

Maggie tucks him in.

>   JACK
> You could love Uganda, Margaret.

His eyes are closed already.

>   MAGGIE
> As I lie down myself to sleep,
> I pray to God my soul to keep,
> If I should die before I wake,
> I pray to God my soul to take.

Jack opens his eyes.

>   JACK
> I think I have come home to die.

25

MAGGIE

Jesus, don't. We can't afford to bury you. I'm glad you're home, Jack. Watch yourself. Go to sleep.

JACK

Aye. Watch yourself. Go to sleep, Okawa.

MAGGIE

What does Okawa mean, Jack?

JACK

Okawa? My houseboy in Uganda. He is Okawa, Maggie.

MAGGIE

Damn it. I thought it was Swahili for gorgeous.

INT. KITCHEN – DAY

Agnes makes tea.

Christina sets up the ironing board. Washed clothes are piled nearby.

CHRISTINA

She's right, you know. Kate's right. I brought shame on this family. Deep shame.

Agnes points her finger at Christina.

AGNES

You brought Michael to this family. And he's not shame. You know that, as does Kate.

ROSE

What's wrong with Jack, Agnes?

AGNES

His nerves.

ROSE

Aye, nerves.

AGNES

We were so proud of him. To have a son a priest. It was a great honour for the whole family. Poor Jack, God help him.

ROSE

Maybe Michael will become a priest, Chris.

AGNES

Maybe.

EXT. GARDEN – DAY

Michael is playing in front of the house.

Kate comes up to him, carrying a paper bag. She watches him playing without saying anything.

KATE

Am I called the gander?

MICHAEL

No, Aunt Kate.

KATE

Who calls me the gander?

MICHAEL

The big fellas do.

KATE

Do you let them?

He turns from her.

Why have you no friends, Michael? You're another gander, aren't you, son?

They look at each other.

I've bought you this. I was saving it for your birthday, but you may as well have it now. Do you know how it goes?

She produces a spinning top from the bag and spins it.

She hears the sound of a motorbike and she looks down the lane.

She sees who is driving the motorbike.

Sacred Heart of Jesus, I don't believe it.

MICHAEL
What's wrong, Aunt Kate?

KATE
(*to herself*)
Our Christina.

EXT. GARDEN – DAY

Kate runs back into the cottage.

EXT. – DAY

Gerry on a motorbike.

INT. KITCHEN – DAY

The sound of the motorbike increases.

Maggie is standing, shocked, as Kate runs in.

ROSE
(*shouting*)
It's him. It's Christina's man. It's Gerry. It's Gerry Evans.

Maggie searches for her good shoes. She looks at herself in a cracked mirror.

MAGGIE
When are we going to get a decent mirror to see ourselves in?

ROSE
You can see enough to do you.

Agnes continues knitting.

Without any sign of emotion, Christina is ironing priest's vestments.

KATE
You're not going to meet him, Christina. You are not going out there to meet that blaggard, Christina.

Christina continues ironing.

Agnes continues knitting.

ROSE
(*screeches*)

Christina, it's Gerry.

CHRISTINA

It must be, yes.

KATE

You're not going to meet that creature.

AGNES

She'll meet him.

KATE

Outside. Not in this house.

MAGGIE

He can stay, Christina.

KATE

He cannot.

Christina puts down the iron.

CHRISTINA

Look at me, Kate, my hands are shaking.

KATE

You will go outside. You will welcome him. And let that be
that.

Kate kisses Christina.

Marconi bursts into song: 'The Isle of Capri'.

EXT. JACK'S BEDROOM – DAY

The music continues.

*Jack is asleep in bed. The bedclothes are dishevelled. He turns in
agitation in his sleep.*

At the window the rooster perches on the ledge.

Jack's face shows distress.

EXT. GARDEN – DAY

The music continues.

The motorbike comes to a stop before the house.

Gerry Evans scans the territory. His eyes meet Michael's eyes.

Michael flees in terror.

> GERRY
> (*whispers*)
> Your mother's son.

Christina walks out to meet him.

He gets off the motorbike.

INT. KITCHEN – DAY

Kate watches through a window.

> KATE
> Look at her now. So calm and beautiful. And when he leaves her, the weeping starts again.

The music stops.

EXT. GARDEN – DAY

Christina stands looking at Gerry.

Gerry and Christina embrace gently.

> GERRY
> How are you, Chrissie? Great to see you.

> CHRISTINA
> Hello, Gerry. How have you been over the past eighteen months?

> GERRY
> Eighteen? Never.

> CHRISTINA
> March last year. March the sixth.

GERRY

Where does the time go?

CHRISTINA

Well, you're here now.

GERRY

Here I am. Wonderful luck.

CHRISTINA

Yes.

GERRY

Is that himself?

Michael peers at them from behind a bush.

He's a big boy.

CHRISTINA

He's growing well.

GERRY

Does he like school?

CHRISTINA

He doesn't say much.

GERRY

Like his Aunt Agnes.

CHRISTINA

Yes, indeed.

INT. KITCHEN – DAY

With the exception of Agnes, who continues knitting, the sisters watch them talking.

KATE

Would someone please tell me what they have to say to each other?

MAGGIE

He's Michael's father, Kate.

31

KATE

That's a responsibility never burdened Mr Evans.

ROSE

Come here till you see him, Aggie.

Agnes continues knitting.

AGNES

Not just now.

EXT. GARDEN – DAY

CHRISTINA

A commercial traveller called into Kate's school last Easter. He'd met you in Dublin. He had some stupid story about you giving dancing lessons up there.

GERRY

He was right.

CHRISTINA

He was not, Gerry.

GERRY

Cross the old ticker. All last winter. Strictly ballroom. Millions of pupils. Everyone wants to dance.

CHRISTINA

Millions of pupils?

GERRY

Fifty-three. I'm a liar. Fifty-one. When the good weather came, they all drifted away. You're the one should have been giving dance lessons. You were far better than me. Do you remember?

He starts to sing 'The Isle of Capri'.

He takes Christina in his arms and they dance.

EXT. GARDEN – DAY

From behind the bush, Michael watches his parents dance.

INT. KITCHEN – DAY

The sisters watch them dance.

Agnes continues knitting.

Gerry's voice can be heard singing.

> MAGGIE
> All he could ever do was dance.

> KATE
> Her whole face alters when she's happy, doesn't it?

Agnes puts down her knitting and joins her sisters at the window.

EXT. GARDEN – DAY

Christina and Gerry finish their dance and laugh, still in each other's arms.

> CHRISTINA
> What brings you to these parts now?

> GERRY
> To say goodbye.

CHRISTINA

Where are you heading for?

GERRY

You'd like to know?

CHRISTINA

I would.

Gerry pats the motorbike.

GERRY

Want a spin on this boy?

CHRISTINA

I might.

GERRY

Get on.

She climbs on the motorbike.

They take off.

EXT. COUNTRYSIDE – EVENING

The camera pans to show the whole landscape.

Gerry and Christina driving through it.

Everywhere there are signs of harvest time, people working in fields, crops ripe and the sun beaming.

EXT. COUNTRYSIDE – EVENING

People working at harvest as sun sets.

EXT. VILLAGE STREET – MORNING

Kate cycles, straight-backed, through the village. Vera McLoughlin's voice stops her.

VERA

Miss Mundy!

Kate stops her bicycle.

KATE

Hello, Mrs McLoughlin. How are you?

VERA

I'm well. I've brought some more wool for Agnes and Rose.
This might be the last batch I give them, God help us all.

Her face crumbles, nearly ready to cry.

KATE

Dear me. What's wrong, Vera? Isn't Agnes the quickest
knitter in Ballybeg?

VERA

You've not heard the word? There's a woollen factory
opening up in Donegal Town, they say. It will be all machine-
knitting from now on.

KATE

Machines? A factory?

VERA

That's right.

KATE

Who says all this?

VERA

It's all everybody's talking about. They're all delighted. Plenty of new work. But what's going to happen to me? I'm too old to go working in a factory. It will be all young ones. You're a lucky woman to have your teaching job.

Vera hands her the wool.

There is a knock from a shop window.

EXT. VILLAGE STREET – DAY

Through the window we see a young girl, Sophia McLoughlin, wave.

VERA

That's our Sophia waving to you. You were her favourite teacher.

INT. SHOP – DAY

At the shop window Sophia whispers to herself.

SOPHIA

That old bitch, the gander.

EXT. VILLAGE STREET – DAY

KATE

Sophia always knew her own mind.

VERA

Who are you telling? Didn't she walk into the house a week ago and tell me she was getting married.

KATE

Married? She's barely sixteen.

VERA

Married. And I'll let her. She'll need a man to keep her. I'll say nothing to Agnes about the factory. Good morning, Miss Mundy.

Vera walks away.

Kate looks angrily through the shop window.

Sophia smiles back at her. A man can be seen behind her.

EXT. A WOOD BY POPPY FIELD

Christina and Gerry together.

The landscape about them is wild and beautiful.

Gerry kisses Christina.

> CHRISTINA
> Where are you going next, Gerry?

> GERRY
> You'll never believe this – I'm going to do a spot of fighting.

> CHRISTINA
> What do you know about fighting?

> GERRY
> I'm a Welshman – we're always fighting.

> CHRISTINA
> You're as soft as butter, Gerry Evans.

He grows serious.

> GERRY
> I'm going off to Spain.

She is shocked.

> CHRISTINA
> Spain?

> GERRY
> The International Brigade. I'm joining up. I'm going to fight against Franco! A company leaves in a few weeks. I'm going to fight for democracy.

> CHRISTINA
> Democracy? Spain? What do you know about Spain?

GERRY

Not a lot. A little. Enough, maybe.

CHRISTINA

Why exactly are you going to Spain, Gerry?

GERRY

Because I want to do something. I want to do anything. With my life. I have to.

CHRISTINA

Then do it.

He kisses her.

He starts to shout 'Then do it.'

He lets out a roar of joy and cartwheels dangerously about the ground.

Gerry, watch yourself. Watch yourself.

INT. KITCHEN – DAY

In the kitchen the fire burns in the range.

Maggie places bread dough into the oven.

She rakes the fire and the flames light her face. Her hands still bear traces of flour dust. She wipes the flour dust into the fire.

INT. SHOP – DAY

The interior of the shop where Sophia works.

It belongs to Austin Morgan, who is serving Kate. Austin is in his forties, a typical Donegal shop-owner, subservient, sly and ambitious. He is also single.

Kate is attracted to him, but she fiercely represses it, only showing it in flashes.

Austin is weighing out the flour.

Sophia is to the edge of the counter, weighing sugar from a large bag into small bags. She watches Kate and Austin intently.

> AUSTIN
> Two pounds of flour, Kate.

> KATE
> Thank you, Austin. And I better not forget the cigarettes, or a certain sister of mine will not speak to me for a week.

> AUSTIN
> Maggie enjoys her wild Woodbine, does she not?

> KATE
> She does indeed, Austin, but God forgive me, I do think it's not a nice habit in a woman.

> AUSTIN
> A harmless enough pleasure, Kate. Now have you got everything? Cornflour, sugar, salt, tapioca – I'm sorry it's gone up a penny.

> KATE
> That's hardly your fault, Austin.

> AUSTIN
> And your radio battery, that's come in from Letterkenny.

39

KATE

Not much good it's going to do in that old set.

SOPHIA

Are you going to the harvest dance this year, Miss Mundy?

KATE

I hardly think so at my age, Sophia.

SOPHIA

Oh, but you should. It will be supreme this year. Supreme.

KATE

Will it be? Will it really be supreme?

She eyes Austin, with a look of irritation at Sophia.

Tea, soap, Indian meal, jelly. How much do I owe you, Austin?

Unseen by Kate, Danny Bradley enters the shop.

Austin and Sophia see him.

Kate notices their change of expression and turns to see him.

KATE

Mr Bradley.

DANNY

Miss Mundy, how are you?

KATE

Very well. And how are you and yours? How is your wife?

DANNY

I no longer have a wife.

KATE

I hadn't heard she'd passed away.

DANNY

She's gone away, to England.

KATE

You should have followed her there. All kinds of things can happen to a body in England. They're not respectable people there as we are in Ballybeg.

40

SOPHIA

Will your sisters be going to the dance, Miss Mundy? Agnes and Rose, will they go?

KATE

No.

Sophia begins to sing in a low voice 'The Rose of Aranmore'.

Kate gives her a look that could kill and snatches her basket of groceries from the counter.

KATE

Would you excuse me? I have an appointment with Father Carlin.

Kate leaves.

SOPHIA

Will you be going yourself, Danny? To the harvest dance? Will you be looking for a new wife?

DANNY

Do you know what you are, Sophia McLoughlin. A dirty cruel little bitch.

He walks calmly out of the shop.

EXT. SCHOOL — DAY

Father Carlin walks towards the door.

INT. SCHOOL — DAY

Kate is waiting in the empty classroom.

There is a map of the world on a wall.

Kate sits in her teacher's chair.

The door opens and Father Carlin comes into the room.

Kate rises to meet him.

Father Carlin does not offer her his hand.

FATHER CARLIN
Miss Mundy.

KATE
Father Carlin, I'm so glad you asked to see me. Father Jack is waiting to meet up with you soon.

FATHER CARLIN
I haven't asked to see you about your brother.

KATE
I was just wondering when you would call out to see him.

FATHER CARLIN
He's not well, I hear.

KATE
He's grand. Thank God, grand. Good feeding and plenty of exercise, he'll be right as rain.

FATHER CARLIN
The rain, yes, that's what he needs.

KATE
Rain?

FATHER CARLIN

The sun in Africa, it would affect anybody. He needs the rain.
That will heal him.

KATE

He's going to say Mass soon.

FATHER CARLIN

I don't think so, Miss Mundy. When he's fit to see people, I'll
call out.

KATE

He's fit to see anybody. Jack is –

FATHER CARLIN

Not well. I know. I know everything about him.

KATE

There is nothing to know.

FATHER CARLIN

I think there is. So do you. You're a smart enough woman.
You must notice things. Have you noticed the numbers in the
school are falling?

KATE

To be honest, Father, I haven't.

FATHER CARLIN

Well, they have. I might need to let a teacher go. That could
be all for the best. You could do with the extra time now you
have Father Jack on your hands. Goodbye to you.

His abruptness hits Kate like a slap across the face.

KATE

I'm a teacher, Father.

Father Carlin is at the door.

What will I do if I stop teaching?

Father Carlin looks her in the eyes and says nothing.

What will become of us?

43

He leaves her in the empty classroom.

EXT. COUNTRYSIDE – DAY

Kate cycles through the landscape. She stops the bike and breathes deeply, looking at people at work in the bog.

One old man greets her.

Her face changes and she feels a moment's peace. She resumes cycling.

EXT. COUNTRYSIDE – DAY

People working on the bog.

EXT. BACKYARD – DAY

Christina washes the dirt off potatoes in an enamel bowl. She throws a potato to Gerry, who catches it.

Michael watches from behind a wall. They see him.

                    CHRISTINA
He's watching you. He's shy of you.

44

GERRY

He'll grow out of it.

CHRISTINA

Will you be here long enough to give him time to grow out of it?

GERRY

I suppose I deserved that. I'm going to buy him a bike.

CHRISTINA

Are you trying to break the child's heart? A bike's what he's always wanted.

GERRY

I will buy him a bike.

CHRISTINA

Don't lie to the child, Gerry.

GERRY

Michael, can I talk to you?

EXT. GARDEN – DAY

Michael remains hidden.

He hears Gerry's voice as he hides.

> GERRY
> (*voice-over*)
> Michael, can I talk to you, son? I need to ask you a question. Will you answer me?

Michael does not answer.

> I'll ask you anyway. What colour do you like best? Black or blue?

Michael is more intrigued but still does not answer.

> I need to know if I should buy you a blue or a black bike.

Against his will, Michael shouts out.

> MICHAEL
> Black.

Gerry faces Christina.

Michael appears from behind the tree.

Michael runs away.

INT. KITCHEN – DAY

Kate looks out the window.

> KATE
> Does Mr Evans ever wonder how Christina clothes and feeds Michael? Does he ask her? Does Mr Evans care? The beasts of the field have more concern for their young than that creature has.

> AGNES
> Do you ever listen to yourself, Kate? You are such a damned righteous bitch! And his name is Gerry. Gerry – Gerry –

She runs out of the back door. Kate calls after her.

Don't I know his name is Gerry . . . What am I calling him –
St Patrick?

                    (she looks to Maggie)

What was all that about?

MAGGIE

Who's to say?

Maggie, putting on her boots, sings in a low voice.

'Twas on the Isle of Capri that he found her,
Beneath the shade of the old walnut tree,
Oh, I can still see the flowers blooming round her,
Where they met on the Isle of Capri.

KATE

If you know your prayers as well as you know those pagan
songs – I am a righteous bitch, aren't I?

Maggie taps her boots on the floor.

MAGGIE

She was as sweet as a rose at the dawning
But somehow fate hadn't meant it to be,
And though he sailed with the tide in the morning,
Still his heart's in the Isle of Capri.

Christina enters.

CHRISTINA

What have you got to sing about?

MAGGIE

Just practising the foxtrot. Where is Gerry?

CHRISTINA

He's with Michael.

MAGGIE

What are they doing?

CHRISTINA

His daddy's giving him a ride on his motorbike.

Maggie and Kate shriek together, 'Motorbike!'

KATE

He'll kill the child.

CHRISTINA

He'll be all right. He's with his daddy.

EXT. COUNTRYSIDE – DAY

Gerry drives the motorbike through the countryside.

Terrified, Michael clings to him.

Gerry kisses Michael's hair.

The boy nearly jumps out of Gerry's embrace.

Gerry stops the bike.

GERRY

What's wrong? Do you not like your daddy to kiss you?

MICHAEL

Are you my daddy?

GERRY

You know I am. I've seen you five or six times. Don't you remember me?

MICHAEL

I've never seen you before this week.

GERRY

You did. Five or six times. You've forgotten.

MICHAEL

Maybe so.

GERRY

Do you see that strange animal over there?

He points to a cow in a field.

MICHAEL

What's strange about it?

48

GERRY

The horn is in the middle of its forehead. Could it be a
unicorn?

MICHAEL

A unicorn's a horse. That's a cow. And there's no horn.

GERRY

Maybe it's invisible.

MICHAEL

It's not there. It's not a unicorn. Could we go home now? I'm
hungry.

GERRY

All right.

Michael suddenly throws his arms about Gerry and kisses his cheek.

What's that for?

MICHAEL

I don't know.

Gerry revs up the bike and drives off.

49

Michael sits, more relaxed, in his arms.

INT. KITCHEN – DAY

Agnes enters with some roses.

> MAGGIE
> Those are beautiful, Agnes.

Jack enters the kitchen. He looks around.

> JACK
> I beg your pardon. My mind was –
> > (*he points at the flowers*)
> What are these?

> MAGGIE
> They're roses, Jack. Flowers.

Agnes hands them to him. He backs away.

> They won't bite you, Jack. They're just flowers.

> JACK
> Yes, flowers.

MAGGIE

I'll put some in your room, with a card under them, saying 'roses', so you'll know what they are.

KATE

Have you taken your medicine, Jack? You're supposed to take it three times a day, you know that.

JACK

One of our priests took so much quinine he became an addict. He almost died. Our local medicine man cured him. There was a strange white bird on my window-sill.

AGNES

That's Rose's pet rooster. Keep away from that thing.

MAGGIE

One of these days I am going to wring its neck.

JACK

In Africa when we want to please the spirits we kill a rooster or a young goat. What is the name of what that is called?
(*he speaks slowly, deliberately*)
A ritual. Ceremony. That's the word I was searching for. I'm so glad I got that.

He shuffles back to his room.

There is an uneasy silence.

KATE

Spirits, medicine man, ritual sacrifices – his head is completely turned.

INT. JACK'S BEDROOM – DAY

Jack has opened one of his trunks. From it he takes a battered triangular hat with three enormous ostrich plumes coming out of the crown.

Christina stands in the doorway looking in.

CHRISTINA

That's a fine hat, Jack.

JACK

It was a present from the District Commissioner. He's a stubborn man. He and I fight a lot, but I like him. He calls me the Irish outcast. When I was leaving he gave me a present of the last governor's ceremonial hat.

CHRISTINA

You must show it to Michael.

JACK

I'll show it to him later.

EXT. COUNTRYSIDE – EVENING

Gerry and Michael drive through the landscape.

Michael wears Gerry's goggles and cap.

INT. THE KITCHEN – EVENING

Christina is making tea. Agnes is setting the table.

AGNES

Is Gerry eating with us?

CHRISTINA

He is, I'm sure.

MAGGIE

We've only a few eggs left and a loaf of soda bread.

Rose comes in.

AGNES

You can smell tea being made a mile away.

ROSE

I can indeed. I saw Michael and Gerry on the motorbike. I'm going to ask Gerry to give me a run on it.

KATE

You'll do no such thing. And why aren't they home yet?

CHRISTINA

They'll be safe.

MAGGIE

Is Gerry all right staying in the barn?

KATE

He's safe staying there.

MAGGIE

Nobody's safe these days. Somebody landed Austin Morgan.
He's getting married next month.

ROSE

Our Kate was fair mad about Austin Morgan. Look at her.
She's blushing, she's blushing.

AGNES

That's enough, Rose.

MAGGIE

And Sophia McLoughlin, that young one, she's to be
married.

KATE

That will put an end to her dancing days. The other day she
had the cheek to ask me if I was going to the harvest dance.
She said it would be supreme this year. Supreme.
(*she takes off her shoes*)
I think I'm getting corns in this foot. I hope to God I don't
end up crippled like poor mother, may she rest in peace.

AGNES

Wouldn't it be a good one if we all went?

CHRISTINA

Went where?

AGNES

To the harvest dance. All dressed up. I think we should all go.

KATE

Have you any idea what it'll be like? Crawling with cheeky
young brats that I taught years ago.

AGNES

I'm game.

CHRISTINA

Oh, God, you know how I loved dancing, Aggie.

KATE

You have an eight-year-old child, have you forgotten that?

Agnes turns to Christina.

AGNES

You could wear that green dress of mine. You have the figure
for it and it brings out the colour in your eyes.
(*to Kate*)
And you look great in that cotton dress you got for
Confirmation last year. You look beautiful in it, Kate.

KATE

This is silly talk. We can't Agnes. How can we?

ROSE

Maggie, will you go with us?

MAGGIE

Will Maggie what? Try to stop me.

KATE

Oh, God, Agnes, what do you think?

AGNES

We're going.

ROSE

We're off. We're away.

CHRISTINA

It costs four and six to get in.

AGNES

I have five pounds saved. I'll take you. I'll take us all. I don't
care how dirty and sweaty those fellows are. How many years
has it been since we were at the harvest dance? I want to
dance, Kate. I'm only thirty-five. It's the festival of Lughnasa.
I want to dance.

KATE

I know, Agnes, I know.

54

AGNES

It's settled. We're going.

CHRISTINA

Like we used to.

ROSE

I love you, Aggie, I love you.

Singing 'Will you come to Abyssinia', Rose starts to do a bizarre and abandoned dance.

Kate panics.

KATE

We're going nowhere. Look at yourselves, will you? Mature women, dancing? What's come over you all? No, we're going to no harvest dance. And you were going to pay for us all out of five pounds you saved. It's more than I have.

AGNES

This isn't your classroom, Kate.

KATE

Maybe I should start knitting gloves.

AGNES

I wash every stitch of clothes you wear. I polish your shoes. I make your bed. We both do, Rose and I. Paint the house, sweep the chimney, cut the grass, save the turf. What you have here, Kate, are two unpaid servants. And if you now will keep your mouth shut, this unpaid servant will make your tea.

Kate is shamed by this. She walks outside.

Maggie looks at Agnes and nods her head.

EXT. GARDEN – EVENING

The day is fading.

Kate stands outside. Maggie joins her.

They hear the sound of Gerry's motorbike in the distance.

> KATE

Mr Evans will be off again for another twelve months.
Christina will sob and lament in the middle of the night. I
don't think I could go through another winter like that.

EXT. COUNTRYSIDE – EVENING

Gerry and Michael are now radiantly happy on the motorbike.

EXT. GARDEN – EVENING

Maggie, for the first time, looks worn out.

> KATE

You work hard at your job. You try to keep the home
together. Then you suddenly realize cracks are appearing
everywhere. I'm going to lose my job, Maggie. They're going
to take away my teaching. Father Carlin's more or less told
me. It's all about to collapse, Maggie.

> MAGGIE
> (*wearily*)

Nothing's about to collapse, Kate.

56

Gerry and Michael drive up on the motorbike.

GERRY

Good evening, ladies. Wow – wow – wow.

He revs the bike.

The other sisters rush outside.

Michael shouts to them.

MICHAEL

Look at me, everybody, on my daddy's motorbike.

Jack shuffles out to see what is going on. He sees the portions of Michael's kite. He picks them up and strikes them together.

They all watch him as he continues to do this.

The beating sticks develop a rhythm.

Jack shuffles, his body slightly bent over, eyes on the ground, feet moving rhythmically. He sings incomprehensibly, almost inaudibly.

KATE

You're dreaming, Jack. Come on, we'll go for our walk.

She takes him by the hand and leads him towards the river.

INT. KITCHEN – NIGHT

The family are finishing a meal in silence. The meal consists of scrambled eggs, toast, tea. There is a bowl of apples on the table.

MICHAEL

What were you doing with the wooden sticks, Uncle Jack?

Christina kicks Michael gently under the table. He looks at her.

Maggie hurriedly speaks.

MAGGIE

Would anybody like more tea?

GERRY

I'm your man, Maggie.

JACK

I was talking to Obi, the Great Goddess of the Earth.

Maggie pours Gerry's tea.

MAGGIE

Is she now?

JACK

At this time of year, at the harvest time in Africa, we celebrate the festival of the new yam, and the festival of the sweet cassava. They're both dedicated to our Great Goddess, Obi –

MAGGIE

Is there a St Obi?

KATE

If there is, she's not in my prayer book.

Agnes takes an apple from the bowl.

AGNES

How do you celebrate it, Jack?

She begins to peel the apple.

JACK

We cut and anoint the first yams and the first cassavas. We pass the bowl around and each takes one.

He takes the bowl of apples and blesses the fruit. He passes the bowl around and each takes one, with the exception of Kate.

We light fires and we paint our faces. Then we dance – and dance – and dance – men, women and children, even the lepers with limbs missing.

MAGGIE

Sacred Heart of the crucified Jesus!

JACK

For days on end, dancing – You lose all sense of time.

MAGGIE

A clatter of lepers doing the military two-step.

CHRISTINA

God forgive you, Margaret Mundy.

JACK

They have a great capacity for fun, for laughing. You'd love them, Maggie. You should come back with me.

MAGGIE

I wouldn't be too keen on the yams, Jack. I'd miss the old spud.

KATE

These festivals, Jack, these aren't Christian ceremonies, are they?

JACK

No. The Ryangans have always been faithful to their own beliefs.

KATE

Will you say Mass soon, Jack? In the house maybe?

JACK

I will. Soon. Monday maybe.

Kate eyes Maggie, who returns the glance.

GERRY

Will I put on the wireless?

MAGGIE

Marconi is in one of his moods.

CHRISTINA

You might have a look at the aerial one of these days, Gerry.

MICHAEL

You'll be able to fix it, Daddy.

GERRY

A bit of music would do us all nicely.

Kate eyes Gerry severely.

KATE

No. We must all be worn out. Good night, Gerry.

Gerry takes his dismissal easily.

> GERRY
>
> Good night, all.

> MICHAEL
>
> Can I stay with Daddy in the barn?

> KATE
>
> No.

> MICHAEL
>
> Please, I want to. Mammy, please –

> KATE
>
> Tonight, Michael, we will all sleep in our own beds. And that is final.

> GERRY
>
> I'll see you in the morning.

He leaves.

There is a short, tense silence.

> CHRISTINA
>
> Come on, Michael. I'll put you to your bed.

> KATE
>
> I'll be in to read to you in five minutes.

> CHRISTINA
>
> No. He'll go straight to sleep tonight. And that too, Kate, is final.

Michael and Christina leave.

EXT. BACKYARD – NIGHT

Gerry walks across the yard to the barn, holding a lamp.

INT. KITCHEN – NIGHT

Maggie starts to clear away the dishes. Rose and Agnes help her.

Maggie sings.

MAGGIE
Oh, play to me, Gypsy,
The moon's high above.
Oh, play me your serenade
The song I love . . .

INT. KITCHEN – NIGHT

The room is in darkness.

INT. JACK'S BEDROOM – NIGHT

Jack sleeps in his single bed.

INT. KATE AND MAGGIE'S BEDROOM – NIGHT

Kate and Maggie sleep in their separate beds. Above them there is a picture of the Virgin Mary.

INT. ROSE AND AGNES'S BEDROOM – NIGHT

Rose is asleep in her bed.

In her nightclothes, Agnes sits looking out of the window at the barn where Gerry sleeps.

She hears the front door open and close. She sees Christina, a coat pulled over her nightgown, run to the barn.

She starts to weep, silently, fiercely.

> ROSE
> (*whispers*)
> What were you crying for, Aggie?

> AGNES
> Are you not sleeping, Rose?

> ROSE
> What are you sad about?

> AGNES
> Do you ever want to go away, Rose?

ROSE

Why?

AGNES

Just wanted . . . away?

ROSE

Danny Bradley's asked me to go away. To America.

AGNES

Danny Bradley is no good for you, Rose.

ROSE

He wants to take me to a picnic. Out at Lough Anna. Look
what he gave me.

*From under her pillow, Rose takes out a silver chain in the shape of a
fish.*

I haven't worn it yet. I'm keeping it for when we get out on
the boat at Lough Anna.

AGNES

You're not going, Rose. Promise me you're not.

Rose is silent.

Do you hear me?

ROSE

I hear you. I love you, Aggie. I love you more than chocolate
biscuits.

AGNES

I love you too, Rosie.

ROSE

Aggie, if you ever do go away, you'll take me with you, won't
you?

AGNES

Promise. But it's to be our secret. Our big secret. Promise.

Agnes closes her eyes.

EXT. GARDEN – DAY

A white rooster crows.

EXT. GARDEN – A WEEK LATER

Music.

The work of the house.

Christina, Michael and Gerry throw sods of turf together, making them into a neat stack.

EXT. GARDEN – DAY

Agnes is scything long grass.

EXT. GARDEN – DAY

Rose feeds the chickens.

EXT. GARDEN – DAY

Maggie is beating dust out of a rug. The dust rises.

EXT. GARDEN – DAY

Agnes's scythe cuts through the grass.

INT. KATE AND MAGGIE'S BEDROOM – DAY

Kate throws a white sheet on to an unmade bed.

EXT. GARDEN – DAY

The sheet turns into a tablecloth, laid on the freshly cut grass.

Rose places a bowl with three hard-boiled eggs on the cloth.

Christina places some tomatoes on it.

Maggie carries out a large teapot.

EXT. GARDEN – DAY

The whole family eat, drink and laugh.

EXT. GARDEN – DAY

Michael lies with his head on Christina's lap. Gerry watches them.
Maggie looks lovingly at the three of them.

EXT. GARDEN – DAY

The family are throwing the last of the turf sods on to the neat stack.

EXT. GARDEN – DAY

When the stack is finished, Gerry lifts Michael on to the top of the turf.
Michael roars and dances wildly.

EXT. COTTAGE – NIGHT

Wide shot of cottage including backyard.

INT. KITCHEN – NIGHT

The red poppies in the vase before the Virgin Mary have withered.

INT. KITCHEN – NIGHT

The sisters are looking at a photograph album. They are all laughing.

> MAGGIE
> Jesus, look at me – look at the cut of me.
> *(she points to a photograph)*
> And I thought my hair was lovely. It was like a whin bush.

> AGNES
> Maggie, you were lovely.

> MAGGIE
> God forgive you for mocking, Agnes Mundy.

Rose points to another photograph.

> ROSE
> Who's that, Maggie?

> MAGGIE
> That's Curly McDaid, God rest him.

AGNES

Curly? He hasn't a hair on his head.

MAGGIE

Bald at seventeen. That's why we called him Curly. Kate could tell you about him.

CHRISTINA

Kate, tell all.

KATE

My lips are sealed.

MAGGIE

Mine are not. He had a wild notion about our Kate.

KATE

I had no more interest in Curly McDaid than the man on the moon.

MAGGIE

He was fair mad about her.

KATE

If we're talking about wild notions, what about him?

Kate points to a photograph.

MAGGIE

Brian, Brian McGuinness.

CHRISTINA

He's gorgeous.

KATE

Your sister thought so as well.

MAGGIE

He was a bit like Gerry, Chris. The loveliest dancer.

KATE

Do you mind the time you were robbed? That dance competition?

MAGGIE

You were there, Kate. And I do remember that night, they had a waltz competition.

KATE

I was looking down at poor Curly McDaid's bald head. But Maggie and Brian were beautiful. They should have won.

MAGGIE

Of course, they gave the cup to the two ould ones.

KATE

You should have won, you and Brian.

CHRISTINA

What happened to him?

MAGGIE

Brian went to Australia.

Maggie turns the pages of the album.

INT. KITCHEN – NIGHT

A black and white photograph of Maggie and Brian.

MAGGIE
(*voice-over*)

He wrote. I answered. But Australia's far away. The way things go.

INT. KITCHEN – NIGHT

Maggie closes the album.

MAGGIE

So that's that.
(*she lights a cigarette*)
Will somebody give us a song? Rose Mundy, I call on you. 'Down by the Sally Gardens'.

ROSE
(*sings*)

Down by the Sally Gardens

My love and I did meet,
She passed the Sally Gardens,
With little snow-white feet.

The sisters sing the rest of the song in harmony.

She bid me take life easy,
As the leaves grow on the trees,
But I was young and foolish,
With her did not agree.

EXT. COTTAGE – NIGHT

The exterior of the cottage as they sing.

INT. KITCHEN – DAY

There is an ink bottle and some paper on the kitchen table. Michael sticks a pen with a nib into the ink. He writes carefully on the paper.

INT. KATE AND MAGGIE'S BEDROOM – DAY

Kate sits on the bed, reading a letter. When she finishes reading it, she crumples the paper.

EXT. BACKYARD – DAY

Gerry is washing himself at the basin outside the barn.

Father Jack, wearing the triangular hat, calls to him from the back door.

JACK
Good morning, Gerry. Do you fancy a stroll by the river?

GERRY
I'll be right after you.

He throws away the soapy water from the basin. Father Jack walks away from the cottage.

EXT. BACKYARD – LATER – DAY

Maggie pumps water into two zinc buckets.

EXT. RIVER – DAY

Gerry is now fully dressed in white flannels, white shirt, a striped blazer and a straw hat, and he carries a walking stick. He strolls down to where Father Jack is waiting for him.

>   JACK
> That's a fine hat.

>   GERRY
> Your own is very impressive as well.

>   JACK
> We must do a swap before I go back to Africa.

>   GERRY
> You're going back?

>   JACK
> I may. Soon.

INT. KITCHEN – DAY

Michael is still writing.

Maggie enters with the buckets of water.

MAGGIE

Where's your mammy?

MICHAEL

She's not up yet. She's wild tired.

MAGGIE

Just as well Kate's doing her rounds in the town.
(*she fills the kettle and saucepan on the range from the buckets*)
Are you getting something ready for school?

MICHAEL

I'm not listening.

Maggie sings and does an exaggerated dance across to the table and tosses Michael's hair.

MAGGIE

Beside your caravan
The camp fire's bright,
I'll be your vagabond
Just for tonight.

MICHAEL

Look what you've made me do. You've ruined my letter.

There is a large blot on the paper.

MAGGIE

Who are you writing to? Whoever it is, he'd need to be smart
to read that scrawl.

MICHAEL

It's to Santa Claus.

MAGGIE

In August? At the feast of Lughnasa? Nothing like getting in
before the rush. What are you asking for?

MICHAEL

A bell.

MAGGIE

A bell?

MICHAEL

For my bicycle.

MAGGIE

For your bicycle?

MICHAEL

The bike my daddy's buying me. In Kilkenny. It's coming
next week. A black bike – a man's bike. It's going to be
delivered here to the house. He promised me.

MAGGIE

Well, if he promised you . . . Aren't you the lucky boy?
(*she gathers up the papers*)
Away and write to Santa Claus some other time. On a day
like this you should be running about the fields like a young
calf. Go on.

MICHAEL

I'm not a calf. My name's Michael. Michael Evans.

Michael runs out.

Maggie stares after him.

Christina comes into the kitchen.

CHRISTINA

God, I enjoyed that sleep.

MAGGIE

Did you?

CHRISTINA

Where's Michael?

MAGGIE

Out playing. Imagining he's on his new bicycle.

She eyes Christina.

CHRISTINA

You never know, Gerry might buy it.

70

MAGGIE

It's just as well Michael is blessed with a great imagination.

CHRISTINA

Is there water boiling for tea?

MAGGIE

There will be. And soda bread. If Agnes and Rose have luck with the blackberries, we should have beautiful jam.

CHRISTINA

They're picking blackberries?

MAGGIE

They are. Rose in her Sunday best for some reason. Sit down. I'll make tea.

EXT. COUNTRYSIDE – DAY

The blackberries are in full bloom.

Agnes is picking the fruit and filling her can.

Rose sits on the ground looking at her. She is wearing her good clothes and shoes.

ROSE

Did you hear what I said to Maggie?

AGNES

I did.

ROSE

She said, 'Well, you're a fine lady to go out picking blackberries.'

AGNES

And you said, 'I'm some toff, Maggie. I'm some toff.'

ROSE

I'm some toff.

AGNES

Well, stop being such a toff and give me a hand.

71

ROSE

All right.

Rose rises and starts to pick fruit, filling her empty can.

Agnes falls into a bush.

Rose laughs loudly.

AGNES

Is that all the sympathy I get from you? Pull me out. Look at my hands – all scabbed with briars.

A church bell rings in the distance.

EXT. COUNTRY ROAD – DAY

A church bell sounds more clearly: the Angelus at midday.

Jack stops in his walk with Gerry.

JACK

What's that?

GERRY

It's a church bell, I think. You should know.

JACK

Yes, I should. Now, what's our direction? I want to know exactly where I am going. Then Kate won't have to nag – Nag, that is not a word, is it?

GERRY

Nag – yes, to keep on at somebody.

JACK

Nag. Good. My English is coming back. Do you speak Spanish?

GERRY

Spanish?

JACK

For Spain.

GERRY

No. Not a word. I can ride a motorbike. That will be enough
to get me signed on. I take it you don't approve.

JACK

Why?

GERRY

I'm going to fight against Franco. The Catholic Church and
everything.

JACK

The Catholic Church, yes. Are they for Franco?

GERRY

Yes.

JACK

They would be.

GERRY

You're sharper than you seem.

JACK

Am I? Those church bells, were they ringing for a wedding?
Will they ever ring for you and Christina?

Gerry does not answer.

Good. Better to leave her single than to leave her married.

EXT. COUNTRYSIDE – DAY

*Agnes continues to pick blackberries. One can is full and she has started
to fill the other.*

Rose's can is half full.

ROSE

Aggie, I've a wild pain in my stomach. And my head's
splitting.

AGNES

That's hit you very sudden.

ROSE

It must be that warm sun.

AGNES

Maybe you should go home and have a wee rest.

ROSE

Aye, I think I will.

AGNES

Go straight home.

ROSE

I will, aye.

Rose walks away.

Out of sight of Agnes, she smiles and opens her palm, to show the silver charm (a fish).

EXT. LAKESIDE – DAY

Danny Bradley stands waiting by a boat on the lake. He hears Rose, turns around and smiles.

Rose is coming down the path.

EXT. A LAKE – SILVER WATER – DAY

A blue boat moves through the still waters of Lough Anna.

Danny Bradley rows the boat.

Rose sits in the boat, the same smile on her face, the charm hanging around her neck.

DANNY

Are you my Rose?

She nods happily.

Rosie, Rose, Rosebud. You'll never go away, will you?

ROSE

Did you bring anything to eat? You said we'd have a picnic and I could eat a horse.

From his bag Danny produces two bottles of milk. With a flourish he also produces a packet of chocolate biscuits.

Rose claps her hands.

Chocolate biscuits!

DANNY

The very boys.

Rose lies back contentedly in the boat.

EXT. A MEADOW – DAY

Jack and Gerry sit by a stream near the cottage.

GERRY

I'm not sure why I'm going to Spain. Everybody says it will be all over by Christmas.

JACK

They said the Great War would be over by Christmas. They always say that about wars. They never are.

GERRY

It's for the cause. There's bound to be *something* right about the cause.

Jack looks him straight in the face.

JACK

It's somewhere to go – Spain – isn't it?

Gerry sees Agnes in the distance.

GERRY

There's Agnes ahead of us.
                    (*he calls to her*)
Agnes, wait for us.

Agnes stops in the distance.

EXT. A MEADOW – DAY

Agnes sees them and smiles. She waits.

EXT. A MEADOW – DAY

Gerry begins to run to her, losing the straw hat.

EXT. A MEADOW – DAY

Agnes laughs happily.

> AGNES
> Gerry Evans, you're an eejit of a man.

He chases the hat, catching it with his walking stick.

EXT. A MEADOW – DAY

Jack watches all of this, their closeness dawning on him.

He removes the triangular hat. There is sweat on his brow. He wipes it away.

EXT. A MEADOW – DAY

Gerry places the straw hat on Agnes's head.

> GERRY
> There now. You're even more beautiful.

> AGNES
> A right glamour girl.

> GERRY
> Pretty milkmaid, put down your pails and dance with me –

> AGNES
> Have a bit of sense, Gerry Evans.

> GERRY
> Dance with me, please. Come on.
> > (*he looks into her eyes*)
> Give me your hand.

Agnes puts down her blackberries.

He takes her in his arms and sings.

GERRY

Now anything goes.
Good authors too who once knew
Better words
Now only use four-letter words
Writing prose,
Anything goes.

With style and easy elegance they dance about the garden.

Gerry sings the words directly to her face.

If driving fast cars you like,
If low bars you like,
If old hymns you like,
If bare limbs you like,
If Mae West you like,
Or me undressed you like,
Why nobody will oppose,
When every night the set that's
smart is intruding in nudist parties in studios,
Anything goes.

Music of 'Anything Goes'.

The dance continues.

INT. KITCHEN – DAY

Christina sees all this at the window.

Kate joins her.

KATE

I know you're not responsible for Gerry's decisions, but it would be on my conscience if I didn't tell you how strongly I disapprove of this International Brigade caper in Spain.

CHRISTINA

Would it?

KATE

It's a sorry day for Ireland when we send young men off to fight for godless Communism. I know he'd say it's for democracy.

                    CHRISTINA
Would he?

                    KATE
I'm not going to argue. I just want to clear my conscience.

                    CHRISTINA
And now you've cleared it. Good for you.

She leaves Kate and walks outside.

EXT. THE BOAT AT LOUGH ANNA – DAY

The sky has grown darker.

                    DANNY
Did you enjoy them chocolate biscuits, Rose?

                    ROSE
I did, Danny. Thank you.

                    DANNY
Is that all I'm going to get?

                    ROSE
It is, yes.

DANNY

When my wife left me, I came here to Lough Anna.

ROSE

To go out on the boat?

DANNY

No. To the water. To throw myself in. I didn't.

He starts to rock the boat gently.

Rose rocks with it.

There is a dance tonight in the back hills. Will you come with
me?

ROSE

I have to go home, Danny. They'll be worried.

DANNY

Are you worried, Rose?

He begins to rock the boat more violently.

Rose is growing frightened.

                    ROSE
Danny – Danny – Danny –

Danny is now drenching them both.

                    DANNY
Will you come with me to the dance?

                    ROSE
Yes. Please, stop this.

Danny stops rocking the boat.

                    DANNY
We'll get back to dry land. And you won't leave me, Rose.
You won't.

INT. KITCHEN – DAY

Agnes enters with the cans of blackberries.

                    MAGGIE
Is that a purple stain on your gansey?

                    AGNES
I fell into a bush. Rose nearly died laughing at me. How is she
now?

Maggie and Kate look at her.

Is she still in bed?

                    MAGGIE
Bed?

                    AGNES
She's here, isn't she? She left me and went home to lie down.
She wasn't feeling well.

*Maggie rushes into Rose and Agnes's bedroom, calling out Rose's
name.*

INT. ROSE AND AGNES'S BEDROOM – DAY

Rose is not in the bedroom.

Maggie stands there, shocked.

Christina enters.

> MAGGIE

Have you seen Rose?

Christina shakes her head.

> MAGGIE
> (*whispers to herself*)

Rosie.

INT. KITCHEN – DAY

In the kitchen Kate questions Agnes.

> KATE

When did she leave you?

> AGNES

Three hours ago. She said she felt out of sorts.

> KATE

And she went off by herself, to come home?

> AGNES

That's what she said.

Maggie and Christina enter.

> MAGGIE

She's not in her bed.

> KATE

Start at the beginning, Agnes. What exactly happened?

> AGNES

Nothing 'happened' – nothing at all. We walked to the bushes.
She said out of the blue – I've forgotten what she said.

> KATE

Think.

> AGNES

She said something about the warm sun – she had a sore head

and a sick stomach – she'd go home and sleep for a while. You're sure she's not in her bed? Where is she? What's happening to our Rosie?

KATE

Stop snivelling, Agnes. Did she go towards home?

AGNES

I don't know – I think so.

MAGGIE

Would she have gone into the town?

CHRISTINA

She wouldn't have gone into the town wearing wellingtons.

AGNES

She was wearing her good shoes, and her blue cardigan, and her good skirt.

MAGGIE
(*whispers softly*)
Danny Bradley.

KATE

What?

CHRISTINA

Oh, God, no.

MAGGIE

Danny Bradley. Lough Anna. The back hills.

KATE

What about the back hills?
(*she turns to Agnes*)
What do you know about this Bradley business?

AGNES

No more than any of you.

KATE

You and Rose are always whispering together. What plot has been hatched between Rose and Mr Bradley?

AGNES

No plot. Please, Kate –

KATE

You're lying to me, Agnes. You're withholding. I want the
truth.

AGNES

Honest to God, I've told you all I know.

KATE

I want to know everything you know. Now! I want to –

MAGGIE

That'll do, Kate. Stop that at once.
(she is absolutely calm)
She may be in town. She may be on her way home now. She
may have fainted if she wasn't well. We're going to find her.
(to Christina)
You search the fields on the upper side of the lane.
(to Agnes)
You take the lower side, down as far as the main road.
(to Kate)
You go to the old well and search all around there.

KATE

Jesus Christ, not the well –

MAGGIE

I'll come with you.
(calls out)
Gerry, Gerry.

KATE

Why are you calling him?

MAGGIE

He has a motorbike. He can travel further –

KATE

Not Gerry Evans. If she's mixed up with that Bradley
creature, keep it to ourselves.

MAGGIE

We need him, Kate. Gerry.

KATE

What are we going to do? Rosie, Rosie – what has become of
our Rosie? What will we do.

MAGGIE

Everybody will do as I told them, and Kate, you will do as I
told you.

EXT. FIELDS – EVENING

Christina searches through the fields, running, sweating.

EXT. RUINED COTTAGE IN A FIELD – EVENING

Agnes climbs in despair through it. The evening is turning into night.

AGNES
(*roars*)

Rose! Rose! Rose!

EXT. GARDEN – NIGHT

Jack is watching fires burn in the hills. He calls into the kitchen.

JACK

Michael.

In his pyjamas, Michael comes into the garden. Jack points to the fires.

What are those?

MICHAEL

The Lughnasa fires. People light them and dance and jump
over. One fella called Sweeney fell into a fire. He was nearly
burned to death.

JACK

Lugh – god of light, god of music. I remember.

*He hears the faint beats of a drum. He starts to follow the direction of
the drumbeats.*

Michael calls after him.

MICHAEL

Uncle Jack, where are you going? I'm supposed to be minding you. Uncle Jack?

Jack walks on, oblivious, towards the poppy fields.

EXT. GARDEN – NIGHT

A fox sniffs round the garden, a vixen. It eyes the white rooster. It goes for the rooster.

The kill.

EXT. LANES – NIGHT

Maggie and Kate walk desolate through the lanes.

MAGGIE

We may go home, Kate, and see if the others have found her. She might be at home, having a cup of tea.

KATE

I hope we'll soon have tea to drink. I've had a letter from Father Carlin. I'm not a teacher any more. Decline in numbers. A lie. He thanked me. A lie. A lie. A lie.

EXT. COUNTRYSIDE – NIGHT

Father Jack walks through the landscape. He bends and picks poppies.

EXT. BACK HILLS – NIGHT

Fires burn.

Men and women drink and dance around the bonfire.

Rose and Danny are among them, dancing. Rose is frightened.

Father Jack wanders into the dance, wearing a garland of red poppies.

The crowd grow quiet.

Father Jack looks at them.

Is this Africa?

The crowd starts to laugh.

Rose and Jack see each other.

JACK

Rose?

DANNY

We're getting married, Father Jack. I'm Danny Bradley. I'm going to marry Rose.

He pulls Rose in front of Jack.

There is a wild howl from the crowd of people.

They push Jack, Rose and Danny towards the fire.

Jack roars.

JACK

Obi – Obi – Obi – Obi – Obi –

ROSE

Jack, I want to go home.

JACK

Are these our relations, Rose? Is this your wedding?

ROSE

They're savages. Pagans. They're no connection to us.

DANNY

Will you marry us, Father? Marry me and Rose.

ROSE

I won't marry you, Danny. You're married already.

DANNY

Look what I'll do for you, Rose. Look.

Danny takes a swig of poteen. He roars and jumps over the fire.

The crowd roar their approval.

                    ROSE
I'm going away, Danny.

                    DANNY
Where?

                    ROSE
A secret. Goodbye. We should go home, Jack. These are not
our people.

                    DANNY
Where are you going?

He grabs her.

                    ROSE
I don't know where.

                    JACK
We're just going home.

Danny lets Rose go.

The crowd roar him on.

Jack takes Rose's hand and they walk away from the crowd.

                    DANNY
I'll follow you, Rose. I'll get you.

EXT. BACK HILLS – DAWN

The dying embers of a bonfire as dawn breaks.

EXT. BACK HILLS – DAWN

Rose and Jack walk through the mountain path.

The motorbike sounds. Gerry appears.

                    GERRY
Are you coming home?

Rose nods and they walk together, Gerry pushing the motorbike.

INT. KITCHEN – DAWN

Rose sees the cans of fruit Agnes has gathered. She looks into them.

> ROSE

You got loads, Agnes.

She puts her hand into one of the cans and takes a fistful of berries. She thrusts the fistful into her mouth, then she wipes her mouth with her sleeve and the back of her hand.

As she chews, she looks at her stained fingers. She wipes them on her skirt.

They're nice, Aggie. They're sweet.

Wanting to hug her, Agnes instead catches her arm.

> AGNES

Rose, love, we were wild worried about you. You said you were coming home to lie down –

> CHRISTINA

But you didn't come home, Rosie –

> MAGGIE

Were you in the town?

> AGNES

That's why you're all dressed up, isn't it?

> CHRISTINA

You went into Ballybeg, didn't you?

Rose looks from one sister to another.

She sits down, takes off a shoe and examines it carefully.

> AGNES

We'll go pick some more blackberries next week, Rosie.

> ROSE

All right. I'll lie down for a few hours, but I'll be up to fetch turf in the morning, Maggie.

Rose moves to the bedroom door.

Kate blocks the entrance.

KATE

I want to know where you have been, Rose.

Rose does not answer.

AGNES

Later, Kate, after she sleeps.

KATE

Where have you been, Rose?

ROSE

Lough Anna.

KATE

Where?

ROSE

Lough Anna.

CHRISTINA

Kate, just leave her.

KATE

You walked to Lough Anna.

ROSE

Yes.

KATE

Did you meet somebody there? Had you arranged to meet somebody there?

ROSE

I had arranged to meet Danny Bradley there, Kate. He brought me out in his father's blue boat. It's a very peaceful place up there.
(*she turns to Agnes*)
He calls me his Rosebud, Aggie. I told you, didn't I?
(*to them all*)
Then the two of us went up through the back hills. We must have seen the last of the Lughnasa fires. They are pagans, Kate. I came home with Jack and said goodbye to Danny.

89

(she turns to Kate)
And that's all I'm going to tell you.
(she turns to them all)
That's all any of you are going to hear.

She goes out, her shoes in her hands.

Michael comes into the room.

KATE
What has happened to this house? Mother of God, what has happened to this house?

MAGGIE
It's morning already nearly. We'll get some sleep. Come on, Kitty dear, to your bed.

She leads Kate to her bedroom.

Christina goes to the mantelpiece, searches for and finds one of Maggie's hidden cigarettes. She lights it and draws heavily on it.

AGNES
Maggie will kill you.

Christina does not answer. She draws again on the cigarette.

INT. BARN – DAY

Gerry is lying fully dressed on his makeshift bed. Christina enters.

GERRY
Will you and Michael come away with me?

She looks straight into his face.

All right, I know. Is there nothing I can do?

CHRISTINA
Nothing.

GERRY
I could leave you alone.

CHRISTINA
You could. Soon. Gerry, don't leave me just yet. A few more days. Stay.

They kiss.

INT. KITCHEN – EVENING

Maggie is kneading flour in the kitchen. Christina is bringing turf from the back door to the fire.

Agnes and Rose knit.

Kate reads a book.

>   MAGGIE
> Where's Gerry?

>   CHRISTINA
> He's trying to fix the aerial.

>   MAGGIE
> That bloody old set was never any good.

>   ROSE
> Never any damned good, that bloody set.

>   CHRISTINA
> He knows what he's doing.

>   ROSE
> Never any damned good, that bloody set.

>   KATE
> You've already offered us that bit of wisdom, Rose.

EXT. GARDEN – EVENING/DUSK

By the chimney, Gerry is fiddling with the radio aerial.

There is a blast of static.

INT. KITCHEN – EVENING/DUSK

The static continues.

The women are looking at the radio.

Music begins. It is barely audible at first, but then it sounds clearly.

It is Irish dance music, very fast and raucous. As the volume increases, we hear the melody.

For a few seconds the women continue their tasks.

Maggie turns around. Her head is cocked to the beat.

She is breathing deeply and rapidly. Her features acquire a look of defiance. She stands still for a few seconds and scatters a little flour.

She opens her mouth and lets out a wild roar.

She begins to dance, arms, hair, bootlaces flying. As she dances, she sings/lilts/shouts.

For a short while she dances alone.

Her sisters watch her.

Rose's face lights up. She suddenly flings away her knitting. She leaps to her feet, shouts and grabs Maggie's hand.

They dance and shout together.

Agnes looks around, leaps up and joins Maggie and Rose, as does Christina.

Agnes, Rose, Christina and Maggie form a circle and wheel round and round. They have their arms tightly around one another's necks and waists.

Kate suddenly leaps to her feet, flings her head back and roars.

Kate dances quickly round the kitchen and out to the garden.

The sisters follow her out, shouting, singing, calling.

EXT. GARDEN – EVENING/DUSK

From the top of the gable end, Gerry looks down at the women dancing.

EXT. BACKYARD – DUSK

Father Jack comes and stands in the back doorway and looks at the women.

INT. KITCHEN WINDOW – DUSK

Michael looks out of the window, half terrified.

EXT. GARDEN – DUSK

As the music and the beat continue to pound, the women continue to dance.

There is a mood of near hysteria.

The women circle and reel.

The music stops abruptly in mid-phrase. Because of the noise they are making, none of the sisters notice.

The dancing continues for a short time.

Kate notices and stops, then Agnes, then Christina and Maggie.

Only Rose continues doing her graceless dance. Then she too notices and stops.

In the silence the women stand where they stop.

The men look at them.

The women gasp for breath.

Short bursts of static emit from the radio.

They look at each other obliquely. They half smile in embarrassment. They feel and look slightly ashamed, slightly defiant.

EXT. THE MEADOW – DAY

Michael saves a penalty from Gerry.

> GERRY
> Soccer's no game for a man. Rugby, that's what Welshmen play. If I had time, I'd teach you to play rugby. You know I'm going away tomorrow. Will you miss me?

> MICHAEL
> Will you miss me? And mammy – will you miss her?

> GERRY
> I will.

> MICHAEL
> Then don't go, Daddy.

> GERRY
> I'm a soldier now, Michael. I have to fight. There's your Uncle Jack. What is he doing in that regalia?

EXT. THE MEADOW – DAY

Jack is walking towards them, dressed in ceremonial uniform. It is very soiled, very crumpled. One of the epaulettes is hanging by a thread. The gold buttons are tarnished.

On his head he wears the tricorn ceremonial hat. It is grubby, its plumage broken and tatty.

Jack carries himself in military fashion, his army cane under his arm.

EXT. THE MEADOW – DAY

Jack has met with Gerry and Michael.

JACK

Gerry, my friend, we must make our formal farewells. I hope all goes well for you in Spain, you old rogue. You're off tomorrow?

GERRY

I am, comrade. That's a wonderful uniform. I could do with that for Spain.

JACK

It was my uniform when I was chaplain to the British army during the Great War. There was a time when it fitted me. There was a time when it was splendid.

GERRY

It still is splendid, Jack.

JACK

But we must make our exchange. The way they do in Africa. I place my possession on the ground.

He places his hat on the ground.

Gerry does likewise.

Now take three steps away from it. Then turn round once.

He does all these things.

So does Gerry.

Now I cross over to where you stand. And you come over to the position I've left.

They do so.

The exchange is now formally and irrevocably complete. This is my straw hat.

He puts it on his head.

And this is your tricorn hat. Put it on.

Gerry does so.

It suits you. Splendid.

Splendid.

They shake hands.

They walk away, arms linked, Michael looking after them.

INT. KITCHEN – EVENING

Vera McLoughlin is in the kitchen.

VERA

I'm broke to the bone arriving like this at teatime, but I had to tell you, it's definite.

The women say nothing.

I have to pay yous off. There's no more need for home-knit gloves. The factory's definitely starting in Donegal Town.

AGNES

How are we going to live, Vera?

VERA

Yous may apply for a job in it. I wish yous better luck than I had. They told me I was too old. I'm forty-one. They said I was too old.

She is near to tears.

Forty. One.

AGNES

It was good of you to come and tell us.

VERA

I only wish it was better news. Good night to yous.

They all answer 'Good night.'

Agnes's face is expressionless. She looks at Rose.

KATE

I'll make the tea this evening. Sit down, Agnes.

AGNES

Right. Right you be, Kate. I'll sit down.

EXT. COTTAGE – EVENING

Vera leaves.

INT. KITCHEN – NIGHT

They are sitting quietly around the fire.

Marconi is playing 'The Homes of Donegal'.

Agnes lets it play for a while, then gets up and switches it off.

AGNES

I can't stick that song.

MAGGIE

Rosie, I was thinking we might get another rooster for you.

ROSE

It doesn't matter.

MAGGIE

And I'll put manners on him early.

ROSE

I don't want another.

CHRISTINA

Where's Jack?

KATE

He's out looking up at the moon and stars. Let him. His own distinctive spiritual search.

MAGGIE

Agnes, do you know what I'm thinking? What has Ballybeg not got that Ballybeg needs?

AGNES

What?

MAGGIE

A dressmaker! So why doesn't Agnes Mundy, who has such
clever hands, why doesn't she dressmake?

AGNES

Clever hands?

Maggie is looking around for her cigarettes.

MAGGIE

You'd get a pile of work. You'd make a fortune.

AGNES

Some fortune in Ballybeg – from stitching shrouds.

MAGGIE

Then how are you going to manage?

KATE

She'll manage. We'll pull together. The family will always
manage.

AGNES

You're right, Kate. We will manage. We always do, don't we,
Rosie? And you know how?

ROSE

How?

AGNES

Our secret. Don't you remember?

ROSE

That's right, Aggie. The secret.

KATE

Which is?

AGNES

Just a secret.

She smiles at Rose.

INT. KITCHEN – DUSK/NIGHT

It is dead of night. The kitchen is empty. Fully dressed, Agnes and Rose enter carrying one suitcase.

Agnes places a note on the table. She opens the door and Rose leaves.

Agnes looks about the empty kitchen. There is a holy-water font at the door. She places her fingers in the font and blesses herself with water. She throws holy water about the house, saying as she does so:

> AGNES
> Kate, Maggie, Christina, Michael, Jack, Gerry.

She walks out of the door and closes it.

INT. KITCHEN – DUSK/NIGHT

The kitchen is empty.

> MICHAEL
> (*voice-over*)
> We never saw them again. They vanished without trace.

EXT. A COUNTRY ROAD IN DARKNESS – DUSK/NIGHT

Rose and Agnes walk through the dark landscape, hand in hand, Agnes carrying a suitcase.

> MICHAEL
> (*voice-over*)
> Years later I learned that they ended as shadows on the streets of London, scraping a living together, dying alone.

INT. BARN – NIGHT

Gerry sleeps in the makeshift bed.

> MICHAEL
> (*voice-over*)
> My father did go to Spain and was wounded. He wasn't shot. He fell off his motorbike. My Aunt Kate said it would put an end to his dancing days. Maybe it did.

INT. CHRISTINA AND MICHAEL'S BEDROOM – NIGHT

Christina sits at the window, looking into the night.

> MICHAEL
> (*voice-over*)
> My mother got a job at the factory. She hated it all her life.
> And my father wrote to her – occasionally.

EXT. FIELDS – DUSK/NIGHT

Jack looks at the sky.

> MICHAEL
> (*voice-over*)
> My Uncle Jack lasted as long as he could, believing to the end
> in the earth and the stars.

INT. KATE AND MAGGIE'S BEDROOM – NIGHT

Maggie sits on the edge of her bed, smoking.

> MICHAEL
> (*voice-over*)
> Through it all Aunt Maggie tried to keep the house going.
> She tried to pretend nothing had happened, but the family
> had changed. It had changed for ever.

INT. ROSE AND AGNES'S BEDROOM – NIGHT

Kate sits on Rose's bed, nursing a pillow.

> MICHAEL
> (*voice-over*)
> And my Aunt Kate was inconsolable. Inconsolable.

> KATE
> Rose – Rosie.

Kate weeps violently, clutching the pillow.

INT. CHRISTINA AND MICHAEL'S BEDROOM – NIGHT

Michael lies asleep.

MICHAEL
(*voice-over*)

Me, I was waiting to become a man. Waiting to get – to get
away. Just to go away. But the memory of that summer is like
a dream to me, a dream of music that is both heard and
imagined; music that seems to be both itself and its own echo.
When I remember it, I think of it as dancing. Dancing as if
language has surrendered to movement.

EXT. GARDEN – EVENING/DUSK

The women dance, ecstatically, in silence.

They continue dancing as Michael speaks.

MICHAEL
(*voice-over*)

Dancing as if language no longer existed, because words were
no longer necessary.

EXT. A FIELD – DUSK/NIGHT

The women raise their hands to the sky.

EXT. THE SKY – MORNING

The kite flies free in the blue sky.